WRITING MYSTERIES

A Take-Action Workbook

Saugeen Publishers
Kitchener, Ontario

Copyright © 2019 by Heather Wright.

All rights reserved. No part of this publication may be reproduced, distributed or transmitted in any form or by any means, including photocopying, recording, or other electronic or mechanical methods, without the prior written permission of the publisher, except in the case of brief quotations embodied in critical reviews and certain other noncommercial uses permitted by copyright law. For permission requests, write to the publisher, addressed "Attention: Permissions Coordinator," at the address below.

Heather Wright
hwrightwriter@gmail.com
http://www.wrightingwords.com

Book Layout ©2013 BookDesignTemplates.com
Cover photo by Steve Buissinne at Pixabay

Writing Mysteries: A Take-Action Workbook
Heather Wright
Saugeen Publishers
ISBN: 978-0-9948671-8-6

The best time to plan a book is while you're doing the dishes.

                        Agatha Christie

I do have fun writing, and a long time ago, I told myself, 'You've got to have fun at this, or it'll drive you nuts.

                        Elmore Leonard

Contents

How to Use This Book	1
Characters	5
Motive, Means, Opportunity, Alibis	39
Plot Planners	49
The Killer's Point of View	51
The Detective's Point of View	57
Chapter-by-Chapter	63
Setting	79
Journal Pages	89
Calendar	151
Coloring & Doodling Pages	178
About Me	189

HOW TO USE THIS BOOK

You are already doing your research, reading the wonderful books and blogs out there designed to help you write a great mystery novel. You have ideas, notes, reflections, and information that need a home. **This book is your desk-top companion on your mystery-writing journey.**

Well-designed tools created especially for your genre will guide your creativity and keep you inspired. In this workbook, you can record details about your characters, your plot plans, your notes on setting, and anything else you need to regularly refer to as you create your story. This workbook also includes journal pages where you can reflect on and celebrate your work plus a calendar to track your progress.

All your notes, thoughts, questions, planning—all in one place.

Inside this book you will find worksheets, planners, and journal pages to help you develop characters, find your story, and reflect on the process. Use this book to schedule your writing time, beat writer's block with a little coloring, and best of all, get the words on the page as you've been dreaming them.

You can find out more about all my books at your online bookseller or on my website: http://www.wrightingwords.com.

If you find this book of value, **please stop by your online bookseller and leave a review**. I appreciate your time and your honest comments. The series includes:

CHARACTERS

Though many have argued that mystery stories are plot driven, they don't work at all if you haven't created three-dimensional characters for your readers to care about. We know our detectives' names for a reason: Gamache, Galloway, Wallander, Robicheaux, Morse, Dobbs, Warshawski, Reacher, Poirot, Millhone …. The authors did their job and created characters that readers love.

Not all detectives have a Hastings or Watson, but most have someone that they can bounce ideas off even if it's a cat or a ghost—and sometimes it's someone they fall in love with. Along with your detective's character pages, there are pages for their sidekick along with those for the suspects and the victim.

The following planners will help you learn more about your characters' personalities, ambitions, and secrets. I've added a notes page at the end of each planner. As you work on your novel, you will discover more interesting things about your characters, and these pages give you a place to record those inspirations.

The pages following the character templates give you space to clarify the motives, means, opportunity, and alibis for the suspects in your story.

NOTES

Detective's Name _____

Physical description	Job, hobbies, special skills
Secret that character has told no one	One thing that character is afraid of
One thing/person that character would do anything to protect	Attitude toward life, family, friends

Connection to victim	Connection to killer
Connection to suspects	Internal conflict that events in the story make worse or force character to overcome

NOTES

NOTES

Sidekick's Name _____

Physical description	Job, hobbies, special skills
Secret that character has told no one	One thing that character is afraid of
One thing/person that character would do anything to protect	Attitude toward life, family, friends

Connection to detective	Connection to victim
Connection to suspects	Internal conflict that events in the story make worse or force character to overcome

NOTES

NOTES

Victim's Name _____

Physical description	Job, hobbies, special skills
Secret that character has told no one	One thing that character is afraid of
One thing/person that character would do anything to protect	Attitude toward life, family, friends

Connection to detective	Connection to killer

Connection to suspects	Connection to suspects

NOTES

NOTES

Killer's Name _____

Physical description	Job, hobbies, special skills
Secret that character has told no one	One thing that character is afraid of
One thing/person that character would do anything to protect	Attitude toward life, family, friends

Connection to detective	Connection to sidekick
Connection to suspects	**Connection to suspects**

NOTES

NOTES

Suspect 1's Name _____

Physical description	Job, hobbies, special skills
Secret that character has told no one	One thing that character is afraid of
One thing/person that character would do anything to protect	Attitude toward life, family, friends

Connection to detective	Connection to killer
Connection to other suspects	Connection to suspects

NOTES

NOTES

Suspect 2's Name _____

Physical description	Job, hobbies, special skills
Secret that character has told no one	One thing that character is afraid of
One thing/person that character would do anything to protect	Attitude toward life, family, friends

Connection to detective	Connection to killer

Connection to suspects	Connection to suspects

NOTES

NOTES

Suspect 3's Name _____

Physical description	Job, hobbies, special skills
Secret that character has told no one	One thing that character is afraid of
One thing/person that character would do anything to protect	Attitude toward life, family, friends

Connection to detective	Connection to killer
Connection to suspects	Connection to suspects

NOTES

NOTES

Suspect 4's Name _____

Physical description	Job, hobbies, special skills
Secret that character has told no one	One thing that character is afraid of
One thing/person that character would do anything to protect	Attitude toward life, family, friends

Connection to detective	Connection to killer
Connection to suspects	Connection to suspects

NOTES

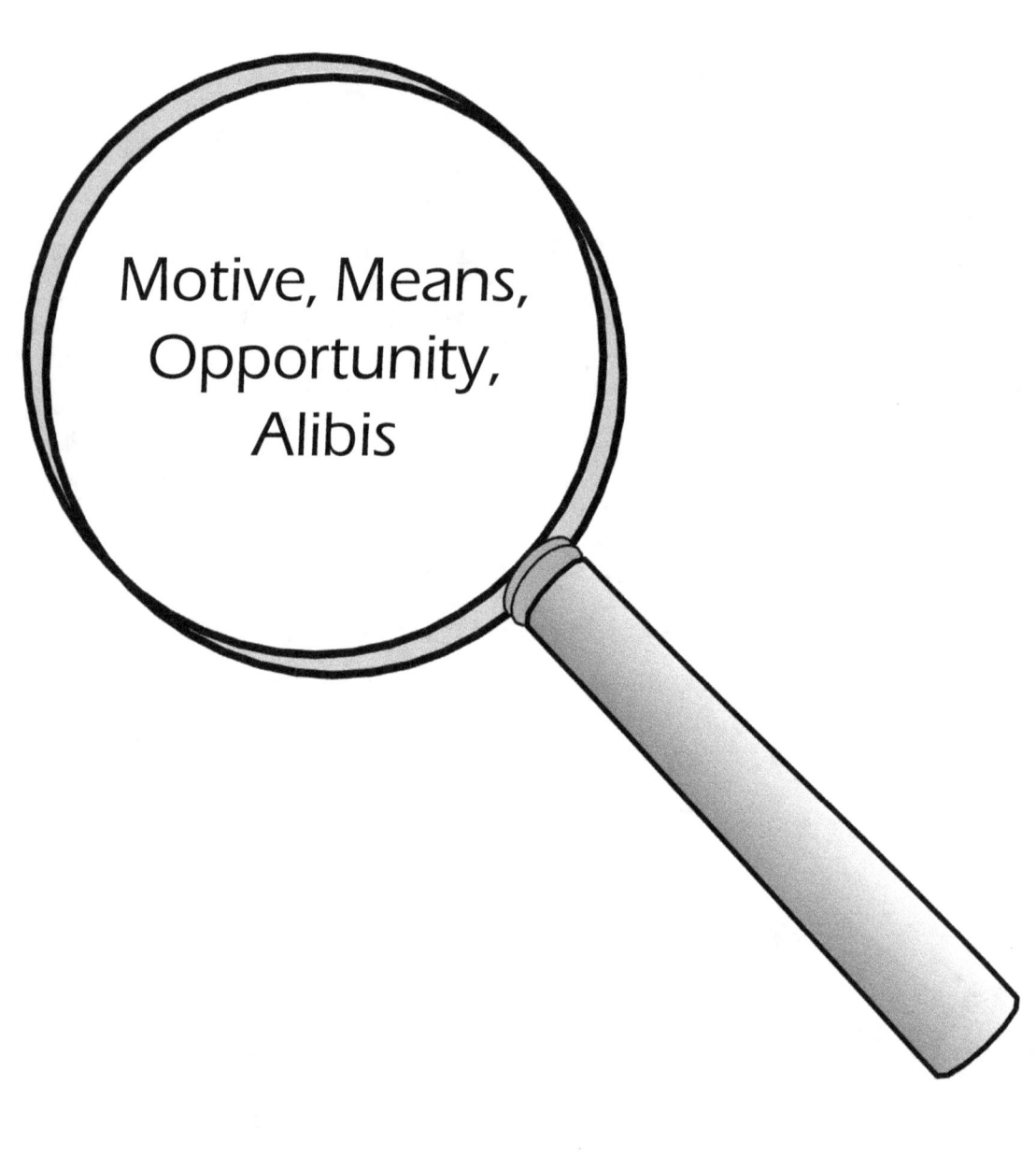

MOTIVE, MEANS, OPPORTUNITY, ALIBIS

PD James, author of 28 books including the Dalgleish novels, described the detective story this way when speaking to Linda Werheimer at NPR in 2009.

> "What we have is a central mysterious crime, which is usually murder. We have a closed circle of suspects with means, motive, and opportunity for the crime. We have a detective, who can be amateur or professional, who comes in rather like an avenging deity to solve it. And by the end, we do get a solution."

At the beginning of your novel, the suspects all must seem to have motive, means, and opportunity. As the novel progresses, the detective will, through questioning, deduction, and research, eliminate them one by one until there is only one possible guilty person.

Until then, building guilty possibilities for your suspects is essential to confuse the reader and the detective until the final piece of the puzzle is put into place. Enjoy!

KILLER _____

MOTIVE	MEANS
OPPORTUNITY	ALIBI

SUSPECT 1 _____

MOTIVE	MEANS
OPPORTUNITY	ALIBI

SUSPECT 2 _____

MOTIVE	MEANS
OPPORTUNITY	ALIBI

SUSPECT 3 _____

MOTIVE	MEANS
OPPORTUNITY	ALIBI

SUSPECT 4 _____

MOTIVE	MEANS
OPPORTUNITY	ALIBI

NOTES

NOTES

NOTES

PLOT PLANNERS

Planning a mystery novel is different from planning other novels because you need to create two stories about the same event. One story is about how the detective solves the mystery, and the other story is about how the murderer plans and carries out the crime.

The first plot planner will help you think about the story from the killer's point of view.

The second planner will help you map the detective's story though the discovery of the murder to the reveal at the end.

A third planner helps you break your story down into chapters.

Why have a plan at all? I always recommend creating an outline for your novel before you begin writing. Unless you have limitless time in which to write, an outline can be your friend. If you know what is going to happen next in your story, you can take advantage of short bursts of time to make progress on your novel.

If you type at 30 words per minute, you can write 450 words in 15 minutes—nearly 2 pages! An outline also ensures that you will get some writing done on those days when the muse is on sick leave or sitting, sulking in the corner and refusing to come out and play.

Conflict is a key element to your plot. Yes, your detective will be in conflict with lying suspects and the killer, but don't forget to give your detective some other problems, too.

Here are some samples:

Person vs. self: What insecurities (can't talk in public, natural shyness) or fears (small places, heights, snakes) does your character have to overcome to succeed?

Person vs. nature: Thunderstorms, ice storms, electrical outages, high winds, poison ivy. They're all out there waiting for your detective.

Person vs. person/society/authority: Not everyone will approve of the detective's actions. How do the people around him or her (her book club, his curling club, the mayor, the police chief, spouses, parents, children, in-laws, etc.) view the detective's involvement?

You learned a lot about your characters in the previous pages. Now is the time to put that information to use as you create the mystery and then unravel it at the end.

THE KILLER'S POINT OF VIEW

Killer's relationship to the victim and the turning point in that relationship that leads the killer to believe that the only solution is the victim's death.

Plan for murder and alibi

Murder 1

Relationship with other suspects – opportunities to divert suspicion – facing the detective

Confidence unravelling – disturbing clue, comment from other suspect, hint from another suspect or detective

Second murder to divert suspicion, cover tracks, eliminate witness

Conflict with detective, lies, cat-and-mouse with detective

Final confrontation with detective and downfall

NOTES

NOTES

THE DETECTIVE'S POINT OF VIEW

Introduction to the detective: Daily life, friends, colleagues, lifestyle

Discovery of body

Questions, conflicts, suspicions, checking alibis

Low Point – another death, arrest of wrong person/friend, realization that was suspecting the wrong person

Conflict, questions, suspicions: more urgency, know killer can kill again, cat-and-mouse with killer

Final confrontation and reveal of killer's identity

Closing action – Wrap up loose ends.

NOTES

NOTES

CHAPTER-BY-CHAPTER

I'm a big fan of Elizabeth Spann Craig's blog, and with her permission, have adapted her tips for plotting a mystery into the following template that divides the action of the novel into 12 chapters. Here's the link to her post on pre-writing: https://elizabethspanncraig.com/uncategorized/pre-writing/.

I encourage you to check out her blog for great tips on creating cozy mysteries, writing, publishing, time management, outlining, and anything else you can think of to help you write a mystery.

NOTES

Chapters 1 and 2

Introduction of all characters—best to start out with sleuth so that reader knows who to identify with right away.
Either a scene showing interaction of future victim and future suspects or introduction of a body.

Chapters 3 through 6

Set up for sleuth's involvement (if an amateur) and then interviewing of suspects. Suspects provide alibis, red herrings, lies, and truths.

Chapter 7

Another body at the book's halfway mark (most of the time) and/or this could also be the time when the wrong person is arrested, adding more urgency to the detective's need to find the real killer.

Chapters 8 through 10

More interviews to follow up on alibis, clues, and to gather information following any second murder. Give suspects opportunity to refute evidence pointing to them from the previous murder.

Chapter 11

Moment of danger for sleuth or moment of increased tension (hostage situation, etc.) indicating story climax. Killer is revealed.

Chapter 12

Sleuth discusses case and clues that helped him/her solve the mystery.

NOTES

SETTING

Even if you are writing about your hometown, you are going to have to do some research. Use the next several pages to record what you do know about your setting, list the questions you need to research, write down any resources, or draw any maps that you may need for reference.

If you are writing an historical mystery, you will need to do even more research. Here is a list of areas to explore.

- Government/ruling class
- Money/how the economy works
- Religious class and power
- Geography
- Climate
- Clothing and how produced/purchased
- Food/diet
- Transportation
- Measures of time and distance
- Communication
- Housing
- Science/Astronomy
- School/training
- Wildlife/vegetation
- Medicine

Also remember to check your diction when writing historical mysteries, so you don't have characters using words that weren't even around at that time. My favourite source for that is *English Through the Ages* by William Brohaugh.

NOTES

NOTES

NOTES

MAPS & DRAWINGS

MAPS & DRAWINGS

MAPS & DRAWINGS

JOURNAL PAGES

Here are 30 days of journal pages for you to record your progress through this book and through drafting your novel. You don't have to write a journal entry every day. Maybe once a week will keep you on track towards your target.

Completing these pages will help you reflect on your process, determine next steps, and record any shiny, do-not-belong-in-this-novel ideas that come to you while you're working on your current project.

When things get tough, or if you feel you are blocked, it's easy to want to drop what you are doing and go with the next shiny thing in your mind. I encourage you to capture these shiny ideas but leave them for later.

Yes, there are writing days when you will feel like you're trying to run uphill in two feet of mud, but those feelings are also part of the writer's life. Every writer faces them—and you are a writer. You can overcome those challenges and reach your goal.

Finishing is your best reward.

Date _____

The Step I Took Toward My Goal

_____
_____
_____
_____
_____
_____
_____

My Surprises, Inspirations, Shiny Things

_____
_____
_____
_____
_____
_____
_____

My Next Steps

To Do (research, word count goals, reading the experts ….)

Date _____

The Step I Took Toward My Goal

My Surprises, Inspirations, Shiny Things

My Next Steps

To Do (research, word count goals, reading the experts ….)

Date _____

The Step I Took Toward My Goal

_____

_____

_____

_____

_____

_____

My Surprises, Inspirations, Shiny Things

_____

_____

_____

_____

_____

_____

My Next Steps

To Do (research, word count goals, reading the experts ....)

Date _____

The Step I Took Toward My Goal

My Surprises, Inspirations, Shiny Things

My Next Steps

To Do (research, word count goals, reading the experts ....)

Date _____

The Step I Took Toward My Goal

My Surprises, Inspirations, Shiny Things

My Next Steps

To Do (research, word count goals, reading the experts ….)

Date _____

The Step I Took Toward My Goal

My Surprises, Inspirations, Shiny Things

My Next Steps

To Do (research, word count goals, reading the experts ….)

Date _____

The Step I Took Toward My Goal

_____
_____
_____
_____
_____
_____
_____

My Surprises, Inspirations, Shiny Things

_____
_____
_____
_____
_____
_____
_____

My Next Steps

To Do (research, word count goals, reading the experts ….)

Date _____

The Step I Took Toward My Goal

My Surprises, Inspirations, Shiny Things

My Next Steps

To Do (research, word count goals, reading the experts ....)

Date _____

The Step I Took Toward My Goal

_____

_____

_____

_____

_____

_____

My Surprises, Inspirations, Shiny Things

_____

_____

_____

_____

_____

_____

_____

My Next Steps

To Do (research, word count goals, reading the experts ....)

Date _____

The Step I Took Toward My Goal

My Surprises, Inspirations, Shiny Things

My Next Steps

To Do (research, word count goals, reading the experts ....)

Date _____

The Step I Took Toward My Goal

My Surprises, Inspirations, Shiny Things

My Next Steps

To Do (research, word count goals, reading the experts ....)

Date _____

The Step I Took Toward My Goal

My Surprises, Inspirations, Shiny Things

My Next Steps

To Do (research, word count goals, reading the experts ….)

Date _____

The Step I Took Toward My Goal

_____

_____

_____

_____

_____

_____

My Surprises, Inspirations, Shiny Things

_____

_____

_____

_____

_____

_____

My Next Steps

To Do (research, word count goals, reading the experts ....)

Date _____

The Step I Took Toward My Goal

_____

_____

_____

_____

_____

_____

My Surprises, Inspirations, Shiny Things

_____

_____

_____

_____

_____

_____

My Next Steps

To Do (research, word count goals, reading the experts ….)

Date _____

The Step I Took Toward My Goal

My Surprises, Inspirations, Shiny Things

My Next Steps

To Do (research, word count goals, reading the experts ….)

Date _____

The Step I Took Toward My Goal

_____
_____
_____
_____
_____
_____

My Surprises, Inspirations, Shiny Things

_____
_____
_____
_____
_____
_____

My Next Steps

To Do (research, word count goals, reading the experts ....)

Date _____

The Step I Took Toward My Goal

My Surprises, Inspirations, Shiny Things

My Next Steps

To Do (research, word count goals, reading the experts ....)

Date _____

The Step I Took Toward My Goal

My Surprises, Inspirations, Shiny Things

My Next Steps

To Do (research, word count goals, reading the experts ….)

Date _____

The Step I Took Toward My Goal

_____
_____
_____
_____
_____
_____

My Surprises, Inspirations, Shiny Things

_____
_____
_____
_____
_____
_____

My Next Steps

To Do (research, word count goals, reading the experts ….)

Date _____

The Step I Took Toward My Goal

My Surprises, Inspirations, Shiny Things

My Next Steps

To Do (research, word count goals, reading the experts ....)

Date _____

The Step I Took Toward My Goal

My Surprises, Inspirations, Shiny Things

My Next Steps

To Do (research, word count goals, reading the experts ….)

Date _____

The Step I Took Toward My Goal

My Surprises, Inspirations, Shiny Things

My Next Steps

To Do (research, word count goals, reading the experts ….)

Date _____

The Step I Took Toward My Goal

My Surprises, Inspirations, Shiny Things

My Next Steps

To Do (research, word count goals, reading the experts ….)

Date _____

The Step I Took Toward My Goal

My Surprises, Inspirations, Shiny Things

My Next Steps

To Do (research, word count goals, reading the experts ….)

Date _____

The Step I Took Toward My Goal

My Surprises, Inspirations, Shiny Things

My Next Steps

To Do (research, word count goals, reading the experts ....)

Date _____

The Step I Took Toward My Goal

My Surprises, Inspirations, Shiny Things

My Next Steps

To Do (research, word count goals, reading the experts ….)

Date _____

The Step I Took Toward My Goal

My Surprises, Inspirations, Shiny Things

My Next Steps

To Do (research, word count goals, reading the experts ....)

Date _____

The Step I Took Toward My Goal

My Surprises, Inspirations, Shiny Things

My Next Steps

To Do (research, word count goals, reading the experts ....)

Date _____

The Step I Took Toward My Goal

_____
_____
_____
_____
_____
_____

My Surprises, Inspirations, Shiny Things

_____
_____
_____
_____
_____
_____

My Next Steps

To Do (research, word count goals, reading the experts ….)

Date _____

The Step I Took Toward My Goal

My Surprises, Inspirations, Shiny Things

My Next Steps

To Do (research, word count goals, reading the experts ….)

CALENDAR

It can take a long time to write a book, so I've included a full year of blank calendars for you to use to track your progress. Since this book contains a collection of your thoughts and plans, it's also a good place to record your word count or time spent writing or whatever you choose to log to keep you inspired by your progress.

Remember, writing in small pieces works, and you have the advantage of having spent time outlining your story. You don't have to wait for the muse to drop by; you know what you are working on next. And you can write out of order, too, if you like. If one scene is really clear in your mind, write it, and put it where it belongs later.

Consider the numbers. If you write 250 words/day (1 page double-spaced) for 300 days a year you will have 75,000 words. Even if you only type at 30 words a minute, 250 words takes less than 10 minutes a day. I find these numbers encouraging—and they also take away the excuse that I don't have enough time to write.

NOTES

Month _____

Sun	Mon	Tues	Wed	Thurs	Fri	Sat

NOTES

Month _____

Sun	Mon	Tues	Wed	Thurs	Fri	Sat

NOTES

Month _____

Sun	Mon	Tues	Wed	Thurs	Fri	Sat

NOTES

Month _____

Sun	Mon	Tues	Wed	Thurs	Fri	Sat

NOTES

Month _____

Sun	Mon	Tues	Wed	Thurs	Fri	Sat

NOTES

Month _____

Sun	Mon	Tues	Wed	Thurs	Fri	Sat

NOTES

Month _____

Sun	Mon	Tues	Wed	Thurs	Fri	Sat

NOTES

Month _____

Sun	Mon	Tues	Wed	Thurs	Fri	Sat

NOTES

Month _____

Sun	Mon	Tues	Wed	Thurs	Fri	Sat

NOTES

Month _____

Sun	Mon	Tues	Wed	Thurs	Fri	Sat

NOTES

Month _____

Sun	Mon	Tues	Wed	Thurs	Fri	Sat

NOTES

Month _____

Sun	Mon	Tues	Wed	Thurs	Fri	Sat

NOTES

NOTES

Image by KaylinArt on Pixabay

Image by KaylinArt on Pixabay

Image by cat_a_pult on Pixabay

Image by KaylinArt on Pixabay

ABOUT ME

I always have more than one work-in-progress. I own too many journals, and I love red licorice, buttered popcorn, and chocolate–not together. I'm grateful for coffee shops where I can go to kickstart stalled projects. I love music, old films, and sing soprano in a choir. (Secret: I leave the really high notes for those who can land them without a squeak.)

I can't imagine my life without writers, watching them become motivated and empowered, and reading the great work that they create. As a coach, I love working one-on-one with writers of all ages. My clients have ranged in age from 15 to 90.

I am also a freelance writer, writing about everything from orchids to wind turbines to weddings to PVC pipe. I have written for national and local publications, and for educational publishers and industry.

My website, **http://www.wrightingwords.com,** hosts my blog and offers links to all my books for writers. You'll also find lots of free resources for writers of all ages and their teachers, too.

If you found this book of value, **please stop by your online bookseller and leave a review**. I appreciate your time and your honest comments.

www.ingramcontent.com/pod-product-compliance
Lightning Source LLC
Chambersburg PA
CBHW080848020526
44118CB00037B/2314